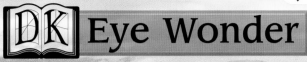

DK Eye Wonder

Rain forest

LONDON, NEW YORK, SYDNEY, DELHI, PARIS, MUNICH, and JOHANNESBURG

Written and edited by Elinor Greenwood
Designed by Tory Gordon-Harris

Publishing manager Mary Ling
Managing art editor Rachael Foster
Jacket design Chris Drew
US editors Gary Werner and Margaret Parrish
Picture researcher Nicole Kaczynski
Production Kate Oliver
DTP Designer Almudena Díaz
Zoology consultant Helen Sharman

First American Edition, 2001

02 03 04 05 10 9 8 7 6 5 4 3

Published in the United States by
DK Publishing, Inc.
375 Hudson Street
New York , NY 10014

DK Publishing offers special discounts for bulk purchases
for sales promotions or premiums. Specific, large-
quantity needs can be met with special editions,
including personalized covers, excerpts of existing guides,
and corporate imprints. For more information, contact
Special Markets Department,
DK Publishing, Inc., 95 Madison Avenue, New York,
NY 10016 Fax: 800-600-9098.

A CIP record for this title is available from the
Library of Congress.

ISBN 0-7566-0096-0

Color reproduction by Colourscan, Singapore
Printed and bound in Italy by L.E.G.O.

See our complete
catalog at
www.dk.com

Contents

Forest facts

- Tropical rain forests only cover a small area of the world (7%).

- Over half the world's wildlife lives in the rain forests.

- The largest area of tropical rain forest is the Amazon jungle in South America.

- Jungle soil is shallow, only 4 in (10 cm) deep, yet some of the tallest trees in the world grow in it.

FRAGILE FORESTS

Rain forests help to clean the world's air and water. Jungle plants give us medicines that make us well when we are ill. Rain forests are very important but are shrinking every day – chopped down for land and wood. We need to value these amazing forests, and take care of all the animals that live in them.

Welcome to the jungle

Monkeys call loudly from giant trees, huge spiders scuttle across your feet, and insects as big as dinner plates buzz around your ears. You're in the jungle!

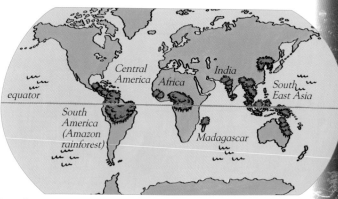

Where in the world...

Tropical rain forests are found on either side of the equator – an imaginary line that circles the globe like a belt. The weather near the equator provides perfect conditions for lush forests to grow.

Weather forecast

It's easy to guess the daily weather forecast in the jungle – hot and humid with heavy rain. Some areas of tropical rain forests get a massive 160 in (4 m) of rain each year, and the temperature is always between 75 and 80 °F (24-27 °C).

Shades of green

Getting lost in the rain forest can be a real problem. The best way to travel through it is by boat. Many rivers snake through the jungle, carrying excess rainwater toward the sea.

Animal magic

There is an incredible amount of different animals living in tropical rain forests. They are mostly very shy, however, and are experts at doing disappearing acts among the leaves.

Baby gorillas, like this one, live with their families in African jungles.

Forest layers

Each animal has its own special place in the rain forest. They may visit their neighbors, or eat out now and then, but they always return home. From the tips of trees to the forest floor, each layer of the forest has a name. Follow this guide to climbing a jungle tree, starting from the bottom.

The crown of an emergent tree can spread to be the size of two football fields.

Emergent trees can be 200 ft (60 m) high.

Storms and high winds lash at the treetops.

Bright green, red, and blue parrots swoop around the treetops.

Emergent layer

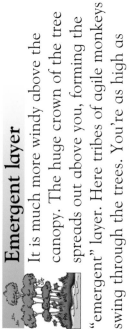

It is much more windy above the canopy. The huge crown of the tree spreads out above you, forming the "emergent" layer. Here tribes of agile monkeys swing through the trees. You're as high as a church steeple so don't look down!

The canopy

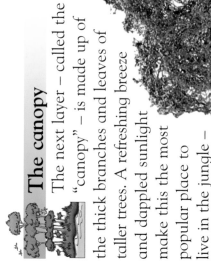

The next layer – called the "canopy" – is made up of the thick branches and leaves of taller trees. A refreshing breeze and dappled sunlight make this the most popular place to live in the jungle – more wildlife lives

Forest facts

- The canopy is like a leaky roof – it stops most rain from reaching the forest below.

- No one knows much about the jungle treetops. They are hard to study because they are so high up.

The understory

Leafy bushes and the tops of small trees make up the first layer, called the "understory." It is dark and hot here, like on the forest floor. Tiny frogs hide in the leaves, and sparkly birds hover in front of flowers.

The forest floor

The climb starts at the leafy forest floor. A soft carpet of dead leaves is perfect for insects. Anteaters and other insect-munching creatures live here.

Rivers

It is impossible to travel far in the rain forest without crossing one of the many streams and rivers that slice through it. Watch out for crocodiles and deadly piranha fish as you cross!

The variety of life

There is more variety of wildlife in the world's tropical rain forests than anywhere else on Earth. There is so much, in fact, that scientists believe there is still a lot to find.

Rainbow birds

Birds of every color flash among the trees. This toucan uses its fantastic beak to crack open the many forest fruits, attract toucan friends, and scare away enemies.

Forest layers are one of the reasons there is so much variety – life is piled on top of life.

Mammals with moustaches

The rain forests support many amazing mammals too, like this emperor tamarin. Mammals are hairy animals that feed their babies with milk.

Teeming with bugs

There are far more creepy crawlies than anything else in the animal kingdom, and nowhere is that more obvious than in the rain forests. On just one jungle tree, scientists found 200 different types of ant – that's more than in many countries.

The postman butterfly is one of 2,000 species of butterfl found in the Amazon jun

New types of insect
are found every day
in tropical rain forests.

Woody words

Carnivore A meat eater.
Poison arrow frogs eat insects
so they are carnivores.

Herbivore A plant eater.
Leaf-munching iguanas and
nectar-drinking butterflies
are herbivores.

Omnivore A meat and
plant eater. Toucans and
tamarins, for example, eat
a mixture of fruit and insects.

Scaly reptiles

Reptiles live at every
level of the jungle,
from big iguanas like
this one, to hissing
snakes and clever
crocodiles. Reptiles
have scales on
their skin and
lay eggs.

*Reptiles are close
relatives of the
dinosaurs – that's
why some of
them look
fierce!*

Amphibians

Brightly colored frogs,
like this poison arrow
frog, are common in jungle
trees. Frogs and toads are
amphibians, which means
they can live in and
out of water.

Giant trees

The giants of the jungle, the emergent trees stick their huge heads out above the canopy. These trees, which start life as tiny saplings on the forest floor, are often hundreds of years old.

Spreading out

Once a young tree has grown past the canopy, it can spread out its branches and enjoy the sunshine. No other giant trees can grow nearby because there is not enough room.

Some of the 200-ft (60-m) high giant trees are up to 1,400 years old.

Wriggly roots

Huge roots, known as buttress roots, wriggle across the forest floor. They make a steady base for the giant trees. These roots also draw up water and nutrients from the top, most

Knee-high saplings need sunlight to grow taller.

Starting out

When an old tree crashes to the ground, it makes a clearing. Saplings now have the sunlight they need to grow. They race toward the light, competing to

Woody words

Sapling A very young tree.

Nutrients The "food" dissolved in water that helps plants grow healthily.

Fertile Rich in nutrients. Plants and trees grow more quickly and strongly in fertile soil.

Piggyback plants

Some canopy branches are like long, thin gardens. They are covered with plants, called epiphytes, growing piggyback on the bark. These plants absorb water from the air, or catch it for themselves, to survive. The epiphytes in this picture are called bromeliads.

Epiphytes can be so heavy that an old tree can't bear the weight and falls over.

Dead leaves mix with water to make a soupy mulch for the plant to draw up.

Bromeliads catch water like buckets. Animals like this tree frog collect around the mini-ponds.

The roots of bromeliads are only for gripping on. They do not steal nutrients from the tree.

Jeepers creepers

Creeper streamers hang between trees, and bright red flowers dot the greenery like party decorations. From orchids to rafflesia, rain forests are home to over half the world's plant life.

Orchids

Delicate and exotic orchids perch high on the branches of tall trees. These epiphytes (see page 11) need to be able to absorb water very quickly in order to survive.

Can you spot the orchid mantis in the flower? It is lying in wait to catch visiting insects.

Lobster claws

On a walk through the Amazon jungle, you are likely to see one of the 450 species of heliconia, also known as lobster claws. These striking flowers love the tropical heat and damp conditions of jungle life.

A stinking giant

A 3-ft (1-m) wide rafflesia bloom – the biggest flower in the world – opens in the dead of night and lasts for only one week. It stinks of rotting meat, earning it the nickname "corpse flower."

Thick woody creepers called lianas stretch between trees.

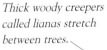

A deadly trap

Insects have a fatal attraction to the sweet nectar in pitcher plants. When they land on the rim, they lose their footing, fall inside, and drown in the fluid at the bottom. The plant then absorbs nutrients from their dead bodies.

Rafflesia have no leaves or greenery. They are parasites, draining all the nourishment and support they need from a host vine.

Pencil erasers, bike tires, and bouncing balls come from rubber trees that were originally found in the Amazon jungle. Two hundred years ago, Europeans flocked to the Amazon to make their fortunes from rubber. Despite it being illegal, they smuggled some trees out to South East Asia. Today, most rubber comes from there.

In the treetops

The animals of the emergent layer make their homes at the very top of the forest. They need a remarkable sense of balance as well as a good head for heights – it's a long way down!

Mighty morphos

Airplane pilots flying above t̶ Amazon often notice the b̶ shimmering wings of mor̶ butterflies below them. Morphos are very fast ̶ agile flyers – easy to s̶ but hard to catch.

Big ears

This common marmoset (a type of monkey) is the size of a squirrel. It is small enough to dart among the trees, catching̶ insects, frogs, and lizards.

Colugo cradle

When it's time to move on, t̶ baby colugo scrambles out of̶ mother's cradling arms and ̶ her back. Mom then uses the̶ flaps on her sides to make ski̶ wings to glide down to lower trees.

ky diver

ne colobus monkey performs spectacular
aps between trees. Its feathery tail helps
steer its jumps as well as slow it down in
the air. It will fearlessly dive
down 30 ft (9 m) – the
height of a two-
story house
– to a
lower tree.

*'obus
nkeys rarely,
ver, go down
he ground.*

Roosting roos

Tree kangaroos,
the "monkeys"
of Australasia
(there are no
wild monkeys in
this area of the
world), can leap
easily between
trees. They have
sharp, curved
claws on their
feet to help
them climb.

*All kangaroos have
babies called joeys.
A mother carries
her joey in a pouch
on her tummy.*

ecause treetop
branches are
thin, many
animals living
here are small
and light.

*—The hairs at the
end of its tail spread
out mid-leap, like
a mini-parachute.*

Forest facts

● Jungle animals do move
between layers, and may travel
down (or up) to find food.

● Animals living in the
treetops have to put up with
a lot of rain and storms.

● Many amazing birds
also enjoy the view
from the treetops.

Flying nutcrackers
Macaws, like the ones
flying in this flock,
have powerful beaks
to break open nuts. To
them, biting into a nut
is as easy as biting into
a banana. They are
very brightly colored
birds and the largest
of all the parrots.

Flying high

There are many different types of birds living in the emergent layer, from majestic eagles and vultures, to noisy gangs of colorful parrots.

Parakeets, along with lorikeets and macaws, are a type of parrot.

Screeching parakeets

It's hard to see this parakeet when it's feeding on fruit or flowers among the leaves. You can't miss it calling to its friends, though.

Rainbow colors

A very fast bird, this rainbow lorikeet will fly a long way to find food. They usually travel in chattering flocks of 15-20 birds, but sometimes flocks join up and hundreds fly together.

Philippine eagles grow to 3 ft (1 m) tall, and 17 lb (8 kg) in weight – they're definitely not as light as a feather!

Jungle cleaner

King vultures help keep the jungle clean by eating dead animals. They find rotting bodies by following other vultures or using their strong sense of smell.

King vultures have bald heads for delving into carcasses.

One fifth of all the birds in the world live in tropical rain forests.

Monkey eater

This rare Philippine eagle is one of the world's biggest eagles. It has broad, rounded wings to help it swoop among the branches of trees and pick off unlucky monkeys.

Tree houses

It's bedtime in the forest. Whether it's a daytime nap or a full night's sleep, every animal needs a safe and comfortable place to rest. Many bed down in the trees.

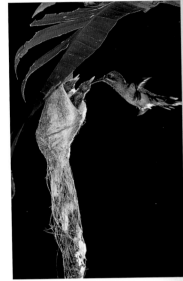

Palaces for ants

The interconnecting chambers of ant plants make ideal living rooms for countless ants. They use the chambers like a palace, with rooms for nurseries, pantries, supplies – and even a special bedroom for the queen.

Spider silk is sticky, so the bird can attach her nest to a leaf. She adds a few twigs to the bottom so that it doesn't blow away.

Soft as silk

Hermit hummingbirds are too small and delicate to make their nests out of twigs. Instead they gather spider silk with their beaks and weave it into a silken cup for their tiny chicks.

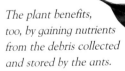

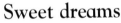

The plant benefits, too, by gaining nutrients from the debris collected and stored by the ants.

Sweet dreams

Tree frogs, tasty snacks for many predators, like to rest inside snug bromeliads. The thick leaves protect and hide them.

Tree frogs also save on water loss by sleeping through the hotter daylight hours.

nest of leaves

angutans learn at a young age how to make
eping nests in the trees. They copy their parents,
ion for action, until they can build their
sts in just a few minutes. They bend back
nches to make their bed and then
tle down comfortably for the night.

*Orangutans
are the largest
tree-dwelling
animals in
the world.*

*This lucky
colugo has found
a suitable hole high up
in the emergent layer.*

Hole owners

There can be fierce competition for tree holes in
the rain forest. Many animals and birds that can't
make the holes themselves prefer to raise their
families in the comfort and safety of a tree hole.

19

A sloth's coat is full of caterpillars that feed on green algae growing in its hair.

Hanging out

Sloths spend their lives hanging upside down. They have strong, hooked claws at the ends of their fingers, like coat hangers (because of these, they can't stand or walk). They move around the trees very slowly. Once a week they climb down to the forest floor to go to the bathroom. It takes them about an hour to get there.

This snake gently wraps its coils around sleeping prey...

...and then tightens its grip.

Canopy creatures

More wildlife lives among the thick leaves and winding branches of the canopy than anywhere else in the rain forest. Monkeys chatter, reptiles flourish, and strange creatures cling to overhanging branches.

Like their namesakes, squirrel monkeys are very agile and speed through the canopy.

Mischievous monkeys

These fun-loving common squirrel monkeys like to live in big groups of 30 or more friends and family. They eat fruit, birds' eggs, and wouldn't say "no" to a nice, juicy spider, either.

Gentle giant

A green iguana looks fierce, but it is really very timid. Even though it can be as long as a man, it will run away at the smallest fright. Iguanas are good climbers, with powerful toes and sharp claws for holding onto branches.

Iguanas store fat in their necks for times when food is hard to find.

One long muscle

A green tree python has a nasty way of killing its prey. It uses its muscular body to squeeze to death. By day, it drapes itself elegantly on a branch. By night, it hunts for sleeping monkeys and birds.

These bulges are strong mouth muscles for holding onto prey.

Forest facts

• Canopy leaves can be 13 ft (4 m) long – like huge, green umbrellas.

• Epiphytes (see page 11) growing on a canopy branch can weigh as much as the branch.

• Canopy plants flower at different times. Some plants flower six times a year, others only once in 40 years.

Forest acrobats

Whether they are swingers, jumpers, or gliders, animals travel around the treetops with acrobatic style. They rarely, if ever, miss their footing and fall

Gibbons have excellent color vision and can turn their heads and look behind them.

King of the swingers

Gibbons really know how to swing! They use their extra-long arms to speed through the canopy, reaching a top speed of 35 mph (50 kmph).

A gecko's tail acts as a rudder to direct its glide.

Gliding geckos

This small lizard has webbed feet and flaps of skin on its sides. When it takes off, the loose skin fills with air and it gently glides down to a lower branch.

Night gliding

A sugar glider has a suitable name. It can glide on skin wings, and it loves to eat the sugary sap of eucalyptus trees. A sugar glider can judge a perfect takeoff and landing, even on the darkest of nights.

A twist in the tail

Some monkeys, like this spider
monkey, have prehensile tails.
This means they can use their
tails as a fifth limb to help them
move around and pick things
up – like having an extra arm.

Forest acrobats
learn how to
swing before they
can walk!

*Lianas
grow from
the ground up
into the canopy, using
a host tree for support.*

Forest playground

The forest provides the perfect framework
for acrobats. Woody creepers (called lianas)
are useful for getting around, and canopy
treetops mesh together to create
"highways" between trees. To a
young chimp like this one, the forest
is one big, adventure playground.

TARZAN

Arghararararargh!
Who can forget
Tarzan's cry to his
animal friends! One
of the most famous
stories of jungle
acrobatics is the story of
Tarzan – a lost baby brought
up by apes. Tarzan takes his lead
from his best friend, Cheetah (a
chimpanzee) and swings around
the forest using lianas.

Monkey moms form very close bonds with their babies.

Monkeys can look out for each other more easily in a group.

Monkey troops

Mona monkeys live in troops of up to 20 members and share friendships and family bonds. There is one ruling male in each troop, and he keeps all the females for himself. No other male gets a look.

Apes and monkeys are human beings' nearest living relatives.

Family facts

● In some animal families mom rears the young, in some dad does it, and in others they share the burden. It varies!

● Animals often leave their families when they are adults.

● Animal brothers and sisters play together – and quarrel!

Happy families

Many rain forest animals live together in organized social groups, like our families. This is how they care for each other in the wild.

Tadpole backpack

A poison arrow frog the size of a one penny coin carries her tiny tadpoles to a bromeliad pond. She deposits her load in the water and then visits the tadpoles daily until they turn into frogs.

Hitching a ride

The treetops can be dangerous for playful youngsters, so many parents carry their young on their backs. In silky anteater families, it is dad that does the carrying.

Jungle giants

Elephants lumber through the jungles of Africa in family groups of up to 20. Baby elephants never stray far from their moms.

...ield bugs are very ...usual. Most other ...sects lay their ...gs and then ...ve them.

...good mother

...fter a female shield bug's ...gs hatch, she stands guard ...er her bug babies. They ...ddle beneath her, somehow ...owing that it is dangerous ...venture out alone.

King of the Amazon

The jaguar is the biggest cat in the Amazon jungle. It loves meat and will eat almost any living thing. Jaguars like to prowl the riverbanks and hook out fish with their paws. They also tackle sleeping alligators. No animal is brave enough to take on a jaguar.

Jaguars are good climbers and sleep in branches.

JAGUAR KNIGHTS

The Aztecs were an ancient people who lived near the Amazon rain forest. They were fierce people and were always fighting their neighbors. They admired the hunting skills of the jaguar and gave the name "Jaguar knights" to the best and most fearless soldiers in their armies.

The understory

The understory is lit with a greenish glow, and the air is still, hot, and humid. Lazy big cats slump on branches, brightly colored birds whirr around flowers, and extraordinary lizards search for insect lunches.

Snakessss

Small creatures, like lizards and frogs, share the understory with some dangerous neighbors. Snakes, such as this golden tree boa, lie in wait for passing prey.

Colorful chameleons

Not only do these unusual lizards have colorful markings, but they can also change color. Chameleons darken to merge into their background and hide, or flash a different color to scare away enemies.

A hummingbird's wings beat up to 80 times per second.

The beating of their wings sounds like someone humming a tune.

Flying jewels

Hummingbirds are tiny – the smallest kind is the size of a bumblebee. They hover next to flowers, feeding on a sweet liquid inside called nectar. They lick the nectar up with long tongues that reach to the end of their spiky beaks.

Chameleons can look in every direction by rolling their eyes.

A cool frog

Tree frogs need lots of water, just like pond frogs. During the day, when it is hotter, they hide in damp, leafy hollows to save water. By night, they catch insects with long, quick-action tongues.

The sticky pads on this white-lipped tree frog's toes help it grip onto wet leaves and stems.

Going batty

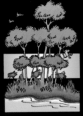

Love them or hate them, bats are common in the rain forest. Bats wake up at night, when the birds go home to roost, and take over their eating grounds.

During daytime, bats hang upside down in caves or trees, sleeping and grooming themselves.

They don't mind crowds, although sometimes squabbles can break out.

Give me a pat!
This doggy-looking bat eats fruit. Also like a dog, it has an excellent sense of smell for sniffing out the juiciest fruits. It spits out seeds or passes them out in its droppings. This helps the spread of fruit trees.

Bats' wings are made of a sheet of thin skin stretched between very long fingers.

Bats are the only mammals that can fly.

Bats and flowers
This long-nosed bat loves sweet nectar, which it licks from inside flowers with its long tongue. Its wings are hairless and as thin as paper. It wraps them around its furry body when it goes to sleep, like a blanket.

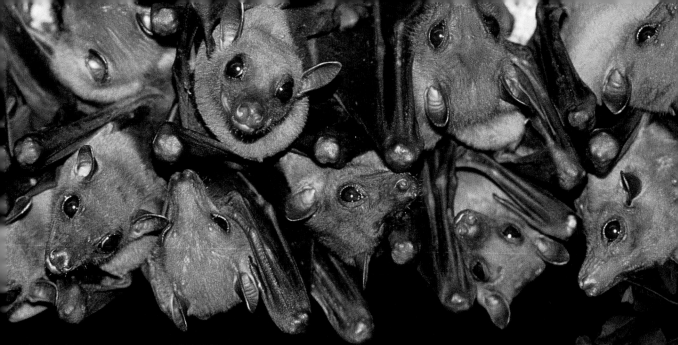

Up, up, and away!

A colony of bats wakes up at dusk. They all take off together with a great flapping of noiseless wings and set off to find food.

At a hidden signal, each bat takes off at the same time.

BATTY SIZES

The biggest bat in the world is the Malaysian flying fox. It can have a wingspan as wide as a car – 5 ft (1.5 m). The smallest bat is the bumblebee bat. It is only 1 in (3 cm) long and weighs 0.05 oz (2 g) – about the size of your big toe.

Vampire bats

This nasty little critter creeps up on sleeping animals and sinks in its fangs. The animal can't feel the bite because the bat has special spit that numbs pain. The bat then laps up blood from the wound.

They drink an egg-cupful of blood each night.

29

Woody words

Camouflage A disguise that makes an animal seem to merge into the background.

Imitation When animals don't look like animals at all, but resemble something their enemies would overlook or never think of eating.

Spot the bug

Can you see the insect in this picture? An insect hunter is sure to overlook this false leaf katydid as it crawls across a tree stump. It even has a hole in its head to make it look like a caterpillar has taken a nibble.

Camouflage

In the jungle, you could be surrounded by animals and not know it. Suddenly, a leaf scurries away or a tree trunk changes shape, and you realize you're being watched...

Thorn bugs

A bird would think twice before gobbling up one of these thorny insects – that's if it knew they were insects in the first place!

Hiding in the shadows

An unsuspecting wild pig could be standing right next to this jaguar and not notice it. The spotted markings on its coat look like the sun shining on shady leaves.

Freeze!

An iguana freezes on a tree trunk, and, as if by magic, almost totally disappears. Its superb camouflage blends its shape into the tree trunk. It is only when the iguana moves that it can be seen again.

Asian leaf frog

A forest floor frog does an amazing impression of a dead leaf. Its pointed snout and hooded eyes add to the leafy effect.

The frog keeps very still and waits for prey to pass.

Lying low

Forest floor animals wind their way between trees across a carpet of dead leaves. The gloom hums with the buzz of insects, and bushes rustle as hidden predators choose their moment to pounce.

Armored armadillos

Giant armadillos (the size of sheep) use powerful claws to dig for insects and worms. Scaly armor protects their backs from big cats as they dig.

Forest facts

- Spiders are not insects. They have eight legs making them "arachnids."

- Armadillos have 100 teeth but they hardly use them.

- Gorillas like to take it easy! They sleep for 13 hours every night and also rest for several hours at midday.

Gorilla picnic

Gorillas live in family groups and work together to protect their territory and young. They sit on the forest floor, eating leaves and grunting to each other. They huff and puff, hiccup, and even burp!

Nothing wasted

Fungi grows easily on the dank, dark forest floor. The air is heavy with the smell of decay as it feeds on rotting leaves.

This stinkhorn is one of millions of fungi that eventually break down dead matter.

Hairy hunters

A curly-haired tarantula as big as a man's fist emerges from its silk-lined burrow after dark. It creeps up on its prey and paralyzes it with a venomous bite. The spider then sucks up the contents of its victim's body.

Insect armies

The jungle is alive with insects as they busily go about their daily tasks. Many live in communities that are similar to armies.

Wasp architects

Paper wasps chew up wood to make strong, light paper. They use the paper to build a cluster of cells for the queen wasp's grubs to live in. Workers collect insects and pieces of caterpillar for the grubs to eat.

Leaf-cutter ants can strip a bush of all its leaves in one night.

Tiny farmers

Leaf-cutter ants carry leaf fragments back to their underground nests. The chewe leaves make ideal compost for growing fungi – the ants' food

Insect army ranks

Queen The only one that lays eggs. The whole insect army serves the queen.

Soldier A defender of the colony, who will fight to protect the nest from attack.

Worker A manual laborer (i.e. builder, farmer, or hunter).

On the rampage

At dawn, worker army ants and some soldier guards set off to hunt, forming a long column that snakes across the forest floor. They attack and kill anything that gets in their way, even large animals.

Blood-sucking mosquitoes lurk in all areas of the jungle. Only females bite, though.

A soldier in defensive position

Ant camp

Army ants make a camp by locking themselves together with their legs and jaws. This solid mass of live ants has their queen and her eggs at the center. When they have stripped the local area of food, the camp moves on.

All worker leaf-cutter ants are female. A few special males and females leave the nest to make new colonies.

Army ants are the most dangerous ants in the world.

Termite builders

As builders, termites are second only to people. They use strong clay to build this amazing umbrella-shaped home. Termites rarely leave their nest since they have everything they need inside.

Hunting

In the rain forest, venturing out to find food is a dangerous job – it's nothing like a trip to the supermarket! You have to be careful *and* lucky. There are traps and ambushes laid everywhere.

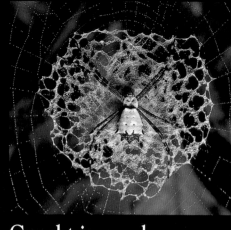

Caught in a web
There are millions of spiders in th[e] rain forest, some as big as your h[and?] Orb weaver spiders catch their pr[ey] in impressive webs like this.

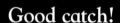

The mantis is weighed down by its fat bottom-half, so it will not overbalance.

Its front feet have spikes to help it hold onto prey.

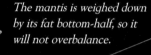

Good catch!
A praying mantis has launched itself toward a passing fly and caught it with its front legs. The fly had no idea it was so close to danger – praying mantises are masters of camouflage.

Poised to strike, eyes ale[rt]

"S" for speed
This poisonous white-lipped tree viper holds the top of its long, slithery body in an S-shape so it can strike out quickly.

Hunting for food? Watch out that you're not someone else's dinner!

Pop eye
This western tarsier looks surprised to have caught such a large moth, but it's thanks to its big eyes that it can see in the dark. Many animals hunt under the cover of night.

The snake's mouth and skin stretch to fit the whole frog into its long tummy.

Frog's legs
A forest floor snake catches a fat frog. Poison in the snake's fangs kills the frog, then the snake swallows the frog whole.

is fearsome viper lies in wait for passing prey.

Timid tapir

A tapir sticks its head out to survey the river scene. Easily startled, this timid vegetarian is an excellent swimmer and can stay underwater for many minutes if it needs to hide from a hungry jaguar.

A tapir's nose is stuck to its upper lip, making a useful trunk for tearing leaves off branches.

River trivia

● Capybaras are the biggest rodents in the world. They are the same size as pigs.

● Female anacondas are five times longer than the males. They can grow as long as 26 ft 3 in (8 m).

Jungle river water is often yellowy-brown and murky.

Riverbanks

Jungle riverbanks are alive with wildlife. Gentle plant eaters browse the thick vegetation, graceful birds show off their fishing skills, and giant snakes lie in wait for passing crocodiles...

Walking on water
This basilisk lizard can escape enemies in a surprising way. Its back feet have long toes with flaps of skin between them so it can skid across the surface of water.

Bird ballet
These elegant great white egrets patiently stalk the river, snapping up frogs and insects as well as fish. At dusk they return to their nests in the trees to roost.

Capybaras eat bankside vegetation.

Giant guinea pigs
Close relations of guinea pigs, capybaras are good swimmers thanks to their partially webbed feet. This makes them clumsy and slow on land, however, like ducks. They live in groups of 10 to 100.

Crocodile for dinner, please!
Anacondas are the biggest snakes in the world, and are one of the few predators of adult crocodiles. An anaconda is capable of squeezing a crocodile to death, then swallowing it whole.

A crocodile meal will satisfy this big snake for about a month.

Watery world

Another, entirely different group of creatures lives in jungle waterways. Many of these are gentle and harmless. Others should be avoided.

Floating gardens

In some places, jungle rivers are slow-moving, shallow, and swampy. These areas are a paradise for plants. Water hyacinths (right) grow quickly, forming tangled rafts on the surface.

Crocodile teeth can only grip and rip. Cro[...] can't chew or munch. The[...] spin in the water to tear o[...] bite-sized chunks.

Shooting fish

Archerfish are very skilled at spitting – they are capable of scoring a direct hit 5 ft (1.5 m) above the surface. The spurt of water knocks an insect into the water where the archerfish gobbles it up.

Trailing, feathery roots absorb nutrients from the water.

These black patches look like shadows from above, so the fish can easily hide.

Amazon manatee

This slow-moving mammal browses through water plants along the mighty Amazon River. It is a sociable creature and usually lives in a small group.

Manatees are often called b[...] their nicknam[...] "sea cows."

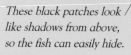

Death roll
A floating log seems to come to life when a caiman lunges at its prey. The struggling beast is held in the croc's jaws and turned around and around until it drowns.

Small but deadly
A school of red piranha fish can tear a large animal to pieces in minutes. They can get into such a feeding frenzy that they take bites out of each other!

Each piranha can only take a small amount of flesh in one bite. They are only successful feeders in large groups.

This is a young spectacled caiman. Caiman are a type of crocodile.

WORLD RECORD HOLDERS
Red piranhas hold the world record for being the most ferocious fish. In 1981, it was reported that piranhas attacked and ate more than 300 people when an overloaded boat sank at Obidos, Brazil. This kind of attack is not common, however!

Jaws
Although this black piranha fish is strictly vegetarian, it is armed with rows of razor-sharp teeth. Indians in the Amazon jungle use piranha jaws as scissors.

41

For many jungle creatures, the Sun going down is an alarm clock to get up. Animals that wake up at night are called "nocturnal" and have special features for survival in the dark.

The jungle is never completely dark. Tiny lights flicker on and off in a beautiful natural light show as fireflies meet up in bushes.

Hide and seek

A jaguarundi has large eyes which help it to see in the dark. These small cats are hard to find in the rain forest. They are excellent climbers and speed around the branches.

Jaguarundis hunt small birds, mice, and lizards that live in the trees.

Toad in the hole

For these toads, life is safer underground or in the dark. They spend the day in a forest floor burrow and come out at night to eat insects.

Fly fishing

Fishing bats don't need to see well since they have amazing hearing. They can "hear" the siz and shape of fish in the river just by sensing the ripples on the surface. They hook fish out with their claws, then kill th prey with their teeth.

Owl butterfly

The spot on this butterfly's wing fools nocturnal insect hunters. In the dark they think it is a beady owl's eye (many small animals prefer to avoid owls!) – rather than the wing of a juicy butterfly.

Butterflies have four life stages: egg, caterpillar, pupa, then butterfly. This leaf could have been eaten by an owl butterfly caterpillar.

Big cats prowl

This Indian tiger is a nocturnal hunter of forest deer and bush pigs. Its long whiskers help it feel its way around, and it can see in the dark five times better than a human being.

Forest facts

● Owl butterflies are as big as dinner plates, with wing spans up to 8 in (20 cm).

● A tiger's roar can be heard 1.5 miles (2.5 km) away – that's very noisy indeed!

● Don't pick a fight with a tiger – they have the strength of 10 men.

● Fishing bats eat while flying or hanging upside down.

Wanted: daredevil scientists!
A brave scientist risks life and limb to explore the top of a tropical rain forest tree. These areas could be home to undiscovered species of plant and animal life.

Collecting bugs
A scientist and student colle and analyze insects. Scientis believe that we have found less than half of the differen types of creepy crawlies livin in tropical rain forests.

Exploring the jungle

The jungle gives up its secrets slowly. After 200 years of study, we still have a lot to discover. We may yet find a cure for cancer, from a plant without a name, in a distant forest.

Amazonian Indians invented hammocks.

In harmony
Jungle people have lived in the rain forest for thousands of years. They know many of its secrets, and can teach us their unique skills and knowledge of the wildlife.

Huge pharmacies
Some ingredients in medicines come from jungle plants. The more we explore the rain forests, the more likely it is we will find plants that can cure serious diseases.

This yam can help people with arthritis.

This hard fruit treats some skin diseases.

Moreton bay chestnut seeds brought hope to people with HIV.

The seeds in this ouabain pod can help treat heart problems.

Rosy periwinkle plants can help treat cancer.

Protecting animals
Some rain forest animals are "endangered," which means there are not very many left in the world. These animals need extra help to survive.

Orangutans are endangered. As a result, orangutan sanctuaries have been set up in jungle areas where they can live undisturbed.

EARLY EXPLORERS
When early European explorers came back from their trips into the Amazon rain forest, they said they had seen men with one leg who could run like the wind, bat people who lived in holes, and beings that were half man, half fish. People outside the forest didn't know what to believe!

Glossary

Here are the meanings of some words it is useful to know when learning about the rain forests.

Amphibian an animal that can live in and out of water.

Arachnid an animal with simple eyes and eight legs, such as a spider.

Bromeliad a type of epiphyte with a rosette of stiff leaves.

Buttress root a root, often growing from the trunk, that helps to keep a tree upright.

Camouflage a color or pattern that matches an animal's surroundings and helps disguise it.

Canopy the thick layer of leaves and branches that form the "roof" of the jungle.

Carnivore a meat eater.

Emergent layer the layer above the canopy made by the crowns of very tall trees.

Epiphyte a plant that grows "piggyback" on another plant, without stealing water or nutrients from it.

Equator an imaginary line that circles the world like a belt.

Fertile (soil) rich in nutrients, where plants can grow more easily.

Herbivore a plant eater.

Imitation when an animal doesn't look like an animal at all, but something its predators would overlook, or never eat.

Insect an animal with three parts to its body and six legs, such as a fly or ant.

Liana a creeping plant.

Mammal an animal that has hair and feeds its young with milk.

Nectar the sweet liquid inside flowers.

Nocturnal active at night.

Nutrients "food" that plants and animals need to grow and live healthily.

Omnivore a plant and meat eater.

Predator an animal that hunts other animals for food.

Prehensile tail a tail that can grasp (like a hand).

Prey an animal hunted for food.

Reptile an animal that has scales and lays eggs.

Rodent a mammal that has long front teeth, like guinea pigs.

Roost to rest or sleep, often in a tree.

Sapling a young tree.

Tropics the hot area that runs around the world in a band, on either side of the equator.

Understory the layer below the canopy, made up of smaller trees and bushes.

Wingspan the distance from wing tip to wing tip.

Animal alphabet

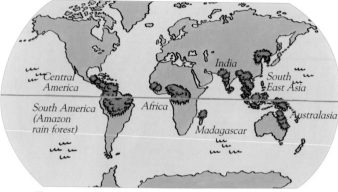

Every animal found in this book is listed here, along with its page number and which area of tropical rain forest it comes from.

Index

Rainbow lorikeet

Useful websites

Animals of the Rain Forest *Jungle animals with bite-sized information and great color pictures.*
www.animalsoftherainforest.com

Toucan Sam's Encyclopedia of the Rain Forest *Everything you need to know, with Toucan Sam as your guide.*
www.toucansam.kelloggs.ca/eng/enter.htm

Zoom Rain Forests *It's all here. Color-in animal printouts.*
www.EnchantedLearning.com/subjects/rainforest

Rain Forest Action Network *Lot of information (and good jungle sound effects), as well as ways to help preserve the rain forests.*
www.ran.org/kids_action/index1.html

Virtual Rain Forest *Find out what's hiding behind the leaves.*
www.msu.edu/~urquhar5/tour/active.html

Acknowledgments

Dorling Kindersley would like to thank:
Hilary Bird for preparing the index; Emily Bolam for original artwork; additional picture researchers, Bridget Tily and Sean Hunter; and Simon Holland for editorial assistance.

Picture credits

The publisher would like to thank the following for their kind permission to reproduce their photographs:
a=above; c=center; b=below; l=left; r=right; t=top;

Ardea London Ltd: Kenneth W. Fink 17cr; **Bruce Coleman Ltd:** 26c, 27bl, 29cl, 29t; Bruce Coleman Inc 12c; Alain Compost 19br; Gerald S. Cubitt 12bl; M.P.L.Fogden 25cr(a); Steven C Kaufman 12cl; Joe McDonald 39tr; Luiz Claudio Marigo 8cr(a), 11br; Rod Williams 17cb; **Robert Harding Picture Library:** 10b, 10t; Frans Lantin/Minden Pictures 23tl; Minden Pictures 33tl; **Chris Mattison:** 36bc; Chris Mattison 30c, 31r; **Minden Pictures:** Mark Moffett 44c; **N.H.P.A.:** 22bl, 28br, 36tr, 42c, 42bc, 43c; G.I. Bernard 31cl; James Carmichael JR 5cl; Planet Earth/Gary Bell 32l; Kevin Schafer 33cr; Martin Wendle 39bl; **Oxford Scientific Films:** 37c; John Brown 39cr; Joe Macdonald 18bl; Partridge Films Ltd 25cl; Philip Sharpe 36tl; P. & W. Ward 14cr; **Planet Earth Pictures:** 27r; Andre Bartschi 16c, 17r; Beth Davidow 9c; Ken Lucas 14c; Florian Mollers 10c; Jonathan P. Scott 15cl; **Plant Pictures World Wide:** 26 background; **Raleigh International Picture Library:** Paul Claxton 44cr(b); **Science Photo Library:** Fletcher & Baylis 13c; Tom McHugh 22l; **Still Pictures:** Andre Bartschi/Still Pictures 5cr; Compost/Visage/Still Pictures 19c; Mark Edwards 40br; Klein/Hubert 15tr; **getty images stone:** Art Wolfe 3r; **Telegraph Colour Library:** J.P. Nacivet 46l; 47r; Planet Earth/Andre Bartschi 31cr(b); Gail Shumway 1c; **Gunter Ziesler:** 18tr; Gunter Ziesler 23r, 32cr(b), 38c, 39cl.

Jacket: **Bruce Coleman Ltd:** Alain Compost br; **Images Colour Library:**